Searchlight
BOOKS™

How
Does Energy
Work?

Investigating
Heat

Sally M. Walker

Lerner Publications Company
Minneapolis

Author's note: The experiments in this book use the metric measurement system, as that's the system most commonly used by scientists.

Lerner Publications Company
A division of Lerner Publishing Group, Inc.
241 First Avenue North
Minneapolis, MN 55401 U.S.A.

Website address: www.lernerbooks.com

Library of Congress Cataloging-in-Publication Data

Walker, Sally M.
    Investigating Heat / by Sally M. Walker.
        p.   cm. — (Searchlight books™—how does energy work?)
    Includes index.
    ISBN 978–0–7613–5773–5 (lib. bdg. : alk. paper)
    1. Heat—Transmission—Juvenile literature. 2. Heat—Experiments—Juvenile literature. I. Title.
QC320.14.W35 2012
536—dc22   2010039515

Manufactured in the United States of America
1 – DP – 7/15/11

Contents

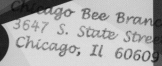

Chapter 1

WHAT IS HEAT?

Heat is important for all animals and plants. Without any heat, living things die. The same thing happens if living things get too much heat. But with the right amount of heat, animals and plants live and grow. Heat from the sun helps keep living things healthy.

If a plant gets too hot or too cold, it dies. But the right amount of heat helps plants grow. What do we call the amount of heat an object has?

Heat is a form of energy. The amount of heat an object has is called its temperature. Water turns into ice at a temperature called the freezing point. Water turns into a gas at a temperature called the boiling point.

This desert is very hot in the daytime. Most plants and animals can't live there because it is too hot and too dry.

Measuring Temperature

We measure temperature in units called degrees. Thermometers are tools that are used to measure temperature.

This thermometer shows the temperature on a warm summer day.

Some thermometers measure temperature with the Fahrenheit scale. Using this scale, the temperature at which water freezes is about 32°F (0°C). And water boils at about 212°F (100°C). Many people in the United States use the Fahrenheit scale.

Other thermometers measure temperature with the Celsius scale. Using this scale, water freezes at about 0°C (32°F). And water boils at about 100°C (212°F). Scientists use the Celsius scale. So do most other people around the world.

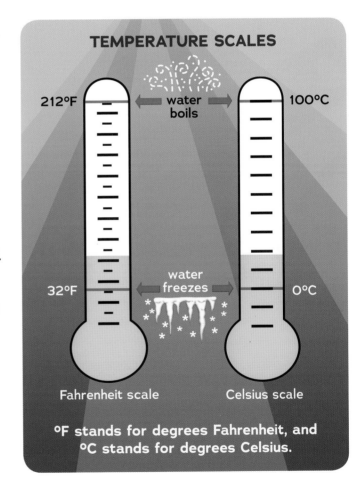

TEMPERATURE SCALES

212°F — water boils — 100°C

32°F — water freezes — 0°C

Fahrenheit scale   Celsius scale

°F stands for degrees Fahrenheit, and °C stands for degrees Celsius.

Kinds of Thermometers

There are many different kinds of thermometers. Some measure the temperature of a room. Some are used to find out if a sick person has a fever. Some are used to measure the temperature of very hot things, such as ovens or melted rocks. And some measure the temperature of cold places, such as freezers.

The thermometer on the left is used when cooking meat. The long metal thermometer is used in making candy. The white plastic thermometer is used to take a person's temperature.

Chapter 2

WHAT MAKES HEAT?

Furnaces and electric heaters heat our homes. Stoves and ovens heat our food. Engines in cars make heat when they run. But where does heat come from? The answer begins with matter.

Toasters use heat to make bread brown and crunchy. What are some other ways that we use heat?

All matter takes up space and can be weighed.

Matter

Matter is anything that takes up space and can be weighed. All the objects around you are made of matter. Books, pencils, air, and milk are all matter.

Matter is made up of very tiny particles called atoms. Atoms are so small that billions of them can fit on the period at the end of this sentence.

THIS ARTWORK SHOWS WHAT AN ATOM LOOKS LIKE. THE PICTURE IS MUCH LARGER THAN A REAL-LIFE ATOM.

More than one hundred different kinds of atoms are on Earth. Each kind of atom is called an element. Oxygen, gold, helium, hydrogen, and calcium are some of the elements.

The dark center part of a pencil is called the lead. Pencil leads are made of an element called carbon.

Atoms can join together to form groups called molecules. Some molecules are made up of only one kind of atom. The molecules found in hydrogen gas are all made of hydrogen atoms.

But most molecules form when different kinds of atoms join together. The combined atoms make a new substance. Two atoms of hydrogen can join with one atom of oxygen. Together they make one molecule of water.

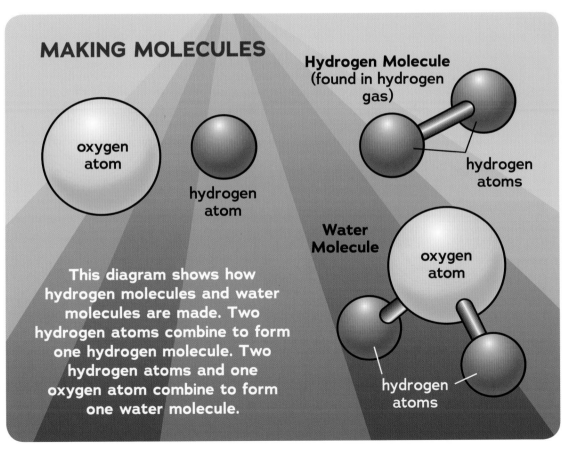

MAKING MOLECULES

Hydrogen Molecule
(found in hydrogen gas)

oxygen atom

hydrogen atom

hydrogen atoms

Water Molecule

oxygen atom

hydrogen atoms

This diagram shows how hydrogen molecules and water molecules are made. Two hydrogen atoms combine to form one hydrogen molecule. Two hydrogen atoms and one oxygen atom combine to form one water molecule.

Atoms and molecules are always moving. When they move, they make heat. You can't see heat. But you can feel it. You can see how it changes the objects around you.

Experiment Time!

Hot molecules move faster than cold molecules. You can prove it. You will need two bowls and some food coloring. Fill one bowl with ice-cold water. Fill the other bowl with very hot water from the faucet. Be careful that you don't burn yourself.

Let the water run a bit before you fill each bowl. It may take a minute or two for the water to become very cold or very hot.

Add one drop of food coloring to each bowl. Do not stir the water. What happens? Does the food coloring spread out faster in the hot water or the cold water? It spreads faster in the hot water.

Add a drop of food coloring to each bowl.

The food coloring spreads out more quickly in hot water (LEFT) than in cold water (RIGHT).

Wait two minutes. Look in the bowls again. The heated water is almost completely colored. The hot molecules are moving fast. So the molecules of food coloring spread out quickly. But not all the icy water is colored. Its cold molecules are moving slowly. It takes much longer for the molecules of food coloring to spread out.

Chapter 3

CHANGING FROM HOT TO COLD

Matter can be hot, cold, or somewhere in between. Touch your tongue. Your tongue is warm matter. Molecules moving inside your body make a lot of heat. That's why your tongue is warm.

Your tongue feels warm to the touch. Do you know why?

An ice cube is colder than your tongue. The molecules in ice barely move. They make almost no heat.

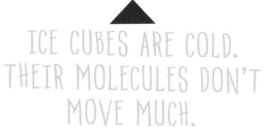

ICE CUBES ARE COLD.
THEIR MOLECULES DON'T
MOVE MUCH.

How Heat Moves

Heat moves from warmer matter to colder matter. When you wrap your hands around a mug of cocoa, heat leaves the cocoa. It moves into your hands. The cocoa becomes cooler, and your hands become warmer.

The opposite happens with a can of cold soda on a hot day. When you put the can against your hot cheek, heat flows away from your cheek. You feel cooler because heat is leaving your cheek. Heat moves from your cheek to the can of soda. The soda and its can become warmer.

Drinking hot cocoa helps you warm up on a cold day.

Chapter 4

HEAT MAKES MATTER GET BIGGER

When matter is heated, it expands. When matter expands, it gets bigger. Gas expands when it is heated. You can prove this.

A popped kernel of popcorn is much bigger than an unpopped kernel. What makes the kernel get bigger?

Testing It Out

You will need a drinking straw and a tall glass. Fill the glass with very hot water from the faucet. Be careful not to burn yourself. Hold your finger tightly over one end of the straw. This stops the air inside the straw from escaping from the hole at that end.

Be sure to keep the end of the straw tightly covered for the whole experiment. If your finger slips, you will need to start over.

Keep your finger over the hole. Dip the other end of the straw into the water. Watch the end of the straw that is in the hot water. Slowly push the end of the straw almost to the bottom of the glass. What happens?

Push the straw down until it almost touches the bottom of the glass.

An air bubble forms at the uncovered end of the straw. When you put the straw in the water, heat from the water warms the air inside the straw. The air starts to expand. It needs more space. But it can't push out of the top of the straw. Your finger is in the way. Instead, the heated air pushes downward into the water.

If you don't see a bubble of air, try again. Make sure the water in the glass is very hot. And don't let your finger slip off the end of the straw.

Leaving Room for Expansion

Solid matter also expands when it's heated. A sidewalk is made of slabs of concrete. You may have noticed that there are spaces between the slabs. In the summer, the sun heats the concrete. The heat makes the sidewalk expand. The spaces give each sidewalk slab room to expand. If builders did not leave the spaces, the concrete would crack.

The spaces between sidewalk slabs give the slabs room to expand.

An Expansion Experiment

Liquid matter expands when it's heated too. You can prove it with an outdoor thermometer and a bowl of warm water. Look at the thermometer's glass tube. At the bottom is a red or silver bulb. Can you see a thin red or silver line inside the tube? It comes up from the red or silver bulb. The color you see is liquid that is sealed inside the tube. How far up the tube does the colored line go?

TAYLOR

°F	°C
120	50
100	40
80	30
60	20
40	10
FREEZE 32	0
20	-10
0	-20
-20	-30
-40	-40

Look for the top end of a thermometer's colored line. The number next to this end of the line is the temperature.

Put the bulb of the thermometer in the bowl of warm water. Watch the colored line. What does it do? The line gets longer. Why? Because the liquid matter inside the tube is expanding. As it expands, the liquid rises higher inside the glass tube.

Some thermometers have a needle instead of colored liquid. The needle moves to point at the temperature.

Chapter 5

HOW HEAT MOVES

Matter conducts heat. This means that matter lets heat move through it. Some kinds of matter conduct heat faster than others. You can prove this yourself.

A metal pan conducts heat quickly. What does it mean to conduct heat?

Experiment Time Again!

You'll need a scissors, aluminum foil, a foam food tray, tape, and a tall glass. Also, ask an adult for a cloth rag that you can cut.

Cut a strip from the foil. The strip should be 3 centimeters wide and long enough to wrap around the glass. Then cut a strip from the cloth rag and one from the foam tray. These strips should be the same size as the foil strip. Tape the three strips around the glass.

Tape the foil, the foam, and the cloth strips around the glass.

Fill the glass with very hot water from a faucet. Be careful you do not burn yourself. Slowly count to fifteen. Then feel each strip. Which strip is hottest?

Carefully fill the glass with hot water.

Touch each of the three strips. Which one feels hottest? Which one feels coolest?

The foil is hottest. Its molecules conduct heat quickly. The cloth strip is warm. Its molecules conduct heat more slowly than the foil does. The foam is coolest. Foam conducts heat very slowly. The reason is that foam has lots of air bubbles inside it. Air conducts heat much more slowly than foil or felt does.

Good and Bad Conductors

Foil is made of a metal called aluminum. Metals are good heat conductors. That is why we use metal pans for cooking. Heat from a stove moves quickly through a metal pan. So the food in a metal pan heats up quickly. That's a good thing when you are hungry.

Foam isn't a good heat conductor. Foam board is often used to wrap houses. The air bubbles in the foam keep heat from moving quickly through it. This helps to keep heated air inside a house. So you stay warmer in cold weather!

Heat moves from warm air into cold drinks. The heat makes the drinks warmer. A foam cooler doesn't conduct heat from the air. So a foam cooler keeps drinks cold.

Chapter 6

HEAT CHANGES MATTER

Matter comes in three forms called states. The three states are solids, liquids, and gases. Wood is a solid. Milk is a liquid. The air we breathe is a gas.

Wood is solid matter. What kind of matter is milk?

Adding Heat

Adding heat can make matter change from one state to another. Adding heat to a solid turns the solid into a liquid. This is called melting. Adding heat to a liquid turns the liquid into a gas. This is called boiling.

ICE MELTS WHEN HEAT IS ADDED TO IT. THE SOLID ICE BECOMES LIQUID WATER.

The inside of a volcano is very hot. It is hot enough to melt solid rock. When the rock melts, it becomes a liquid called magma.

Adding lots of heat to water makes it boil. The water changes from a liquid into a gas called water vapor.

When water becomes very hot, it boils. The liquid water becomes a gas.

Losing Heat

Losing heat can also make matter change its state. When a gas loses heat, it becomes a liquid. As water vapor loses heat, it becomes a liquid. Water is liquid matter.

And when a liquid loses heat, it becomes a solid. If you remove enough heat from water, it freezes. It becomes solid matter called ice.

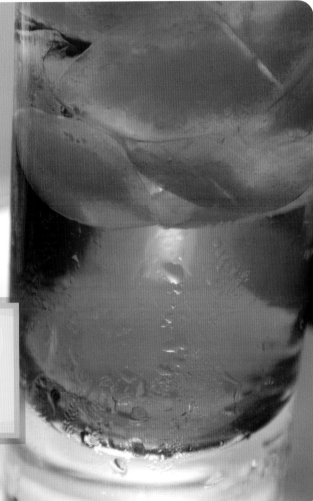

Air contains water vapor. Heat moves from warm water vapor into a cold glass. Water vapor that loses heat changes into drops of liquid water.

CHANGES OF STATE

steam
(gas)

Adding heat to a liquid turns
it into a gas. This is
called boiling.

Taking heat
away from a gas turns
the gas into a liquid. This is
called condensing.

water
(liquid)

Taking heat away from a
liquid turns the liquid into
a solid. This is called
freezing.

ice
(solid)

Adding heat to
a solid turns it into
a liquid. This is called
melting.

Heat from the sun makes a cold day feel warmer.

You have learned a lot about heat. Although you can't see heat, you know it is there. It's inside you and everything you see or touch. Explore your home, school, and neighborhood. Be a heat detective. Look for heat clues in your life.

Glossary

atom: a very tiny particle that makes up all things

boiling: changing from a liquid into a gas

boiling point: the temperature at which water turns into a gas

condensing: changing from a gas into a liquid

conduct: to let something move through. Matter conducts heat.

element: a substance that cannot be broken down into different substances because it is made of only one kind of atom

expand: to become bigger. When matter is heated, it expands.

freeze: to change from a liquid into a solid

freezing point: the temperature at which water turns into ice

gas: a substance that can change its size and its shape. Air is a gas.

liquid: a substance that flows easily. Water is a liquid.

matter: what all things are made of. Matter takes up space and can be weighed.

melting: changing from a solid into a liquid

molecule: the smallest piece of a substance. A molecule is made up of atoms that are joined together.

solid: a substance that stays the same size and the same shape. Wood is a solid.

states: the solid, liquid, and gas forms of matter

temperature: the amount of heat an object has

thermometer: a tool used to measure temperature

Learn More about Heat

Books

Magloff, Lisa. *Experiments with Heat and Energy*. New York: Gareth Stevens, 2010. This book offers more fun heat-related experiments for you to try.

Mahaney, Ian F. *Heat*. New York: PowerKids Press, 2007. Mahaney tells all about heat.

Moore, Rob. *Why Does Water Evaporate?: All about Heat and Temperature*. New York: PowerKids Press, 2010. This selection explores heat and temperature.

Waxman, Laura Hamilton. *The Sun*. Minneapolis: Lerner Publications Company, 2010. This title takes an up-close look at the sun—the source of most of our planet's heat.

Websites

BBC Bitesize Science: Expansion and Contraction
http://www.bbc.co.uk/schools/ks3bitesize/science/chemical_material_behaviour/behaviour_of_matter/revise2.shtml
Learn more about temperature, expansion, and contraction at this interesting website.

How Popcorn Pops
http://www.kidzworld.com/article/547-how-popcorn-pops
Find out how heat makes popcorn pop.

Thermometer
http://pbskids.org/zoom/activities/sci/thermometer.html
Learn how to make your own thermometer.

Index

Photo Acknowledgments

Photographs copyright © Andy King. Additional images in this book are used with the permission of: © Karl Lehmann/Lonely Planet Images/Getty Images, p. 5; © Anthony Berenyi/Shutterstock Images, p. 6; © Andrew Paterson/Photographer's Choice RF/Getty Images, p. 9; © Simone Brandt/Alamy, p. 11; © Chris Harris/All Canada Photos/Alamy, p. 33. Illustrations by © Laura Westlund/Independent Picture Service, pp. 7, 13, 36.

Front cover: © Bronskov/Shutterstock Images.

Main body text set in Adrianna Regular 14/20.
Typeface provided by Chank.